Also by Natasha D. Frazier

Devotionals

The Life Your Spirit Craves

Not Without You

The Life Your Spirit Craves for Mommies

Fiction

Love, Lies & Consequences

Through Thick & Thin: Love, Lies & Consequences Book 2

Shattered Vows: Love, Lies & Consequences Book 3

Copyright © 2017 by Natasha D. Frazier
Published by Encouraging Works
Printed by Lightning Source, Inc.

All rights reserved. No portion of this book may be used in any form without the written permission of the publisher.

Printed in the United States of America.

ISBN: 978-0-9994496-0-8

Scripture quotations are NLT unless otherwise noted. Scripture quotations marked NLT are taken from the Holy Bible, New Living Translation, copyright © 1996, 2004. Used by permission of Tyndale House Publishers, Inc., Carol Stream, Illinois 60188. All rights reserved.
Edited by: Cheryl Molin

Cover design by BJ Benjamin O'Neal (I Imagine Beyond)

For autographed copies, please visit:
www.natashafrazier.com

Note from the Author

I am thankful to my Heavenly Father, who has allowed me the opportunity to do the thing that brings me joy and peace and gives Him glory. This is book number 7! Whoo-hoo!! He has blessed me with the heart to encourage women and the ability to do that through writing. Thank you for entrusting me with such a task. He has also given me a wonderful family who supports my writing career. Eddie, my awesome husband, I love you and appreciate you for all that you do. Thank you for your unwavering support. My babies: Eden, Ethan & Emilyn, mommy loves each of you dearly. To my mom, dad, stepdad and sisters, I thank you for your love and support from afar.

To my special set of girlfriends who push me to go further and have encouraged me from the very start: Tiera, Toccara & Shenitra - I love you ladies and appreciate your friendship.

Readers - Thank you for continuing on this literary journey with me. You each hold a special place in my heart, so please know that with every stroke of the keyboard, I am thinking of you. I hope this book makes you uncomfortable enough to take your life to the next level. (smile)

Much love & many blessings,

Natasha

How Long Are You Going to Wait?

NATASHA D. FRAZIER

Contents

Introduction: The Life Your Spirit Craves

Seek God for Purpose

Life is Choice-driven

Do Not Despise Small Beginnings

The Enemy of Comparison

Seek Counsel

Balancing it All

About the Author

The Life Your Spirit Craves Sample

The Life Your Spirit Craves

In 2012, I published a 30-Day devotional and journal titled, *The Life Your Spirit Craves,* to inspire readers to seek, accept, and pursue their God-given assignment in whatever season of life they happened to be in. Some of us have an inkling of what we should be doing, while others believe God has been silent when it comes to giving them direction. Could it be that you believe you need to be repositioned to be purposeful? New job? New church? New city? New ministry?

Perhaps you already have everything you need within you to walk in purpose. Maybe God has you right where He wants you. Or maybe you haven't done anything with what He's already given you. Whether you're certain of what you should be doing and need encouragement to take the next step or you're still trying to figure out what God wants you to do, keep in mind that in the center of it all is God - if it's from Him, in Him will you find direction.

This book serves as a supplement to *The Life Your Spirit Craves* to help you clarify your assignment and encourage you to get started. At the end of each chapter are a set of scriptures to mediate on and a set of questions to answer. This book will prove to be useful to you if you pray, study the scriptures, answer the questions, and take action. I look forward to hearing how you've stepped out on faith to live the *Life Your Spirit Craves*.

How Long Are You Going to Wait?

So we keep on praying for you, asking our God to enable you to live a life worthy of his call. May he give you the power to accomplish all the good things your faith prompts you to do. (2 Thessalonians 1:11)

SEEK GOD FOR PURPOSE

A little over ten years ago, I sat in a training room full of interns conducting a self-assessment. One of the questions we were asked was, "What are your strengths and weaknesses?" If you're like me, you dread answering this question, because if you're in an interview, the way you answer this question could result in the interviewer passing you up for another candidate. What's worse is that we had to stand in front of the group and give our answer. When it was my turn, I stood with my jittery hands to my side, trying to steady my voice as much as possible and said, "Public speaking is my biggest weakness and I always find myself in a situation where I have to do it." And that was my truth. No matter where I was or what I found myself doing, I had to get up and speak. The mere thought of this made my stomach twist in knots. The moderator looked at me and said, "God may be preparing you for what's to come. Whatever He has for you to do may require you to speak, so don't say that's your weakness." Poor lady didn't understand my plight or maybe it was I who didn't understand. It wasn't that public speaking was a weakness, it was more so the fact that it made me uncomfortable. And many times, that is exactly what happens when God gives an assignment – it's uncomfortable!

Many moons later, I must be honest and admit that I often want to run for cover when I'm asked to speak or share my story, but God never allows me to run and hide in a corner. And because I know what God is leading me to do, how could I allow my fear and discomfort to keep me in my seat? Are you allowing fear of the unknown to keep you in your seat? Does your assignment make you uncomfortable? Good! It should. Or are you still straddling the fence about your next steps? If you are, then this book is the perfect start for you to step out and seek the One who gives purpose, clarity, and direction.

Because our purpose comes from God, it is important to first seek God for what He desires for you in this season of your life, whatever that season is. You see, you may know your purpose, but how you should be carrying it out may be different than how you carried it out last year or how you will need to carry it out a few years from now, and that can cause some level of uncertainty. But our Master knows and can provide the answers you seek. It is important that we are in constant prayer and communication with God to seek His will.

Psalm 37:4 tells us that God will give us the desires of our heart if we delight ourselves in Him. In order to delight in Him, we must learn more about Him, and that is done by spending time in His presence. When we spend time in His presence, inevitably, our desires will begin to match His. Our desires must be in alignment with God's will, and then God will give us the desires of our heart.

Seeking God: What does this look like? Begin with praying and asking God to show you what He wants you to do. I can attest that the Lord will show you if you make yourself available to do His will, and you truly desire Him and His will above all else. Have you already begun praying about it? Can you recall the answers that God has given you, if any? Do you recognize God's voice?

Not only is it important to pray about purpose, but it is imperative that we know how to identify God's voice. How does God speak? God speaks through Scripture and He may give clarity through prayer, and oftentimes through His messengers. When you're concerned about whether or not God is speaking to you, remember two things: God always gives confirmation and God will

How Long Are You Going to Wait?

never move you to do anything that is contrary to His Word and His character.

Study the following Scriptures: John 10; 1 Samuel 3; Isaiah 30:21; John 16:13.

Application

1. Write down a specific prayer asking God to show you what He desires you to do in this season of your life.

2. John 10 speaks about God's sheep being able to discern His voice. Do you have problems with discerning God's voice?

3. In 1 Samuel 3, Samuel was just learning God's voice. Note that Samuel was alone. Do you allow yourself to be alone and in a place without distractions so that you can hear God's voice clearly?

4. Choose a time to seek God alone and meditate on His Word. God will honor the time that you establish to meet Him.

5. What are some things that hinder you from hearing God's voice clearly? (sin, worries, desires of others, fear, etc.)
6. Be honest with yourself and God. Be willing to sacrifice your time for what He is calling you to do.

Ask yourself:

1. Do I truly desire to walk in the purpose that God has for me?
2. What am I willing to sacrifice? (Think temporary satisfaction for the pursuit of purpose.)
3. Are my prayers for purpose specific?
4. In what ways has God answered my prayers to show me my assignments? What actions of faith did I take when God revealed His assignment for my life?

LIFE IS CHOICE-DRIVEN

It's one thing to have a vision, goal or dream that you want to achieve, but it's another thing to actually pursue it. Far too often, we all walk around with ideas buried inside of us and choose not to work to make them a reality because of fear of the unknown, what others may think of us or failure.

It is true we do not know what the future holds, but I can guarantee you that if you never do anything past just thinking or dreaming about your goals, you will never achieve them.

How Long Are You Going to Wait?

One of the most essential elements in pursuing *The Life Your Spirit Craves* is the power to choose. You have free will. Though the vision may have come from God, if you never act upon it, the blessing that you have inside of you will never get to the person who needs it.

Those who know me well know that I talked about writing a book for many years before I actually had the guts to do it. I often think back to January 2009 when I actually put it on paper for the first time as a goal. It wasn't a clear measurable goal; my notepad simply said: Write a book. I was proud of myself, thinking I had done something. In my mind, it was almost as if I'd written a book based on the level of excitement I had.

In January 2009, our pastor preached a series of sermons on purpose and "getting to your address," and my address was writing a book. During that time, our cameras often zoomed in on members of the congregation during worship service. I saw myself on one of the rollbacks of one particular service in January when we were instructed to bring our plans and the pastor would pray over them. I was standing near the front of the sanctuary waving my notepad proudly.

I wrote a couple of pages but that was about the extent of it. I allowed many other things to get in the way, and that prevented me from completing my goal. I often think back to that moment because I did nothing more than write down what I wanted to do, with no plan as to how I was going to get there.

Write It Down

I believe it is very important to write down your goals. I'm not saying this just because I'm an author and enjoy writing; but I truly believe that writing helps the goal setter. Writing things down helps solidify and clarify your thoughts. Writing also holds you accountable.

Don't do as I did back in 2009 and simply write your goal. I encourage you to take it a step further and create actionable plans to help you accomplish this goal. Writing things like, "Start a business," is not going to help you accomplish your goal. Be specific. What kind of business do you want to start? What is it going to take for you to get your business running? What resources do you need? What research do you need to do? When are you going to start making strides to accomplish these things? Set a date.

Giving yourself a deadline is very important because it gives you something to work toward. Be as specific as possible, but also be flexible. These are your goals and it is okay if you don't meet the exact dates that you originally set; make adjustments. The important thing here is that you are working toward bringing your vision to life. You are no longer just dreaming or thinking about it but you are making steps to make it a reality.

The Choice

Even though you may write it down, nothing will happen until you choose to pursue that which God has placed upon your heart. No one can make that decision for you and no one can pursue it on your behalf. Remember that the vision was given to you, so it is up to you to see it to fruition.

Don't be intimidated or discouraged if some people are not excited about this new thing you're embarking upon. Don't even expect everyone to own *your* dreams. Don't allow others' lack of excitement to keep you from being positive and moving with the same vigor you had when you decided to step out in faith to pursue it.

The Wait

When it comes to living a life of purpose, we procrastinate out of concern with how big or small our assignment is, comparing ourselves to others, lack of counsel, time, or other resources, and fear. I will spend the rest of this booklet encouraging you not to let any of those things stop you. Once you decide to move forward, you take action one step at a time to get to the place you're destined to be.

How Long Are You Going to Wait?

Study the following Scriptures: Habakkuk 2; Hebrews 6:11; Proverbs 10:4; 12:24; 21:5; Psalm 119:173.

Application

1. Write down your vision. Be specific.
2. What has stopped you from pursuing this vision?
3. How can you overcome these obstacles?
4. Create a list of actionable steps and goals (measurable, realistic, achievable, time-based) that will position you to get to the place you're trying to go.

DO NOT DESPISE SMALL BEGINNINGS

You'll find in Scripture, Zechariah 4:10, that this is exactly what was instructed of Zechariah: Do not despise small beginnings. In the Scripture text, an angel comes to Zechariah in a vision regarding the rebuilding of the temple. Zerubbabel had begun rebuilding the temple but faced strong resistance from the enemy, but God's mighty hand was at work. To God's people, it may have seemed like the temple would never be rebuilt and that their case was hopeless, but God had other plans. Sometimes it can be tough to visualize the end when the beginning seems so meager, but remember that if God gives a vision, His hand will play a part in making sure it comes to pass; we just have to keep going.

When we first get the vision to accomplish something, we're on fire and ready to take off, not realizing that the vision that we see is not how it begins. It takes much work and energy before the vision comes to pass, and we often become discouraged when we realize that it isn't going to happen in an instant. Maybe you started a business and you're not seeing any profit, or you've written a book and you're having difficulty getting through the marketing process. Perhaps you went back to school and the coursework seems to be even harder than you remembered.

When you actually begin to work out the vision, you may experience a little heartache and difficult situations. That's not uncommon. This is only the beginning, and if you can work past the beginning and keep going, you'll experience the victory that's on the other side of your labor. Let me caution you not to measure your life by human standards. What may seem like failure to us, may not be failure by God's standards. Remember that He loves us and above all else, He desires our hearts. Maybe the other side of your labor won't be earning a living from pursuing your vision, but your reward may be learning to trust God and walk more closely with Him. That's victory, isn't it? Perhaps you will earn some large amount of money or win some prestigious award, but I believe you find fulfillment and bring honor to God by taking a step of faith and pursuing the vision.

Besides, if you give up, you'll never experience the fullness of the vision. Imagine opening a scroll. As you unroll it, you can only see parts of it at a time. Like the scroll, I believe that God shows us bits and pieces of a vision because if He showed us everything, we'd likely become too scared to even pursue anything at all. So before you try to open the entire scroll, seek to attain those things you can see, that is, your current vision.

It Takes More Than One Day

When we conceive a vision, oftentimes we become overwhelmed at the start of pursuing it because we think we have to do it all at once. No one said you have to do it in one day, and I don't believe that God will put that kind of pressure on you. Consider Nehemiah rebuilding the wall of Jerusalem (Nehemiah), the Israelites taking possession of the land God promised their ancestors (Joshua), David learning that he would become king (1 Samuel 16 and 2 Samuel 2), God creating the world (Genesis 1), or the greatest purpose of Jesus' crucifixion and resurrection. In each of these examples, the vision and purpose were clear, but none of them happened overnight. Just because you know what you should do, doesn't mean that it's time to do it.

Prepare yourself. Put together an actionable plan and gather your resources before you jump head first into pursuing the vision that God has given you. It's one thing to know what you should be doing and another thing to actually do it. Don't become overwhelmed by looking at the big picture.

Study the following Scriptures: 1 Corinthians 10:23; Zechariah 4; Colossians 3:23; Hebrews 13:21; Genesis 1.

Revisit:

1. What is my vision?
2. What is my plan to pursue this vision?
3. What are my goals?
4. Are my goals measurable?
5. What resources do I need (time, finances, people, etc.)?

THE ENEMY OF COMPARISON

When you set out to accomplish any task, one of the worst things you can do is compare yourself to another person. Why? Because everyone is different and everyone's journey is different. We are all unique, and as the Bible puts it, "fearfully and wonderfully made" (Psalm 139:14).

Comparison is an attack of the enemy and causes us to quickly lose focus. When you compare, you're not concentrating on your goals; you're too busy trying to understand how and why things are working the way they are for the next person. We have to be mindful that the assignment is not about us, but God using us so that others can get what they need.

Let's say your vision is to write a book. There is nothing wrong with studying the business and craft of other authors to get an understanding and learn more about the industry, trends, etc. However, the issue comes when you're so busy focusing on what another author is publishing or marketing that you cannot focus on the book you're supposed to be writing. You've become caught up with coveting their success, and now you can't pursue your own. The same is true for anything that you start: business, ministry, or restaurant. You begin comparing your journey to theirs, and that can be detrimental to you and your vision. No one else's journey will be the same as yours. You don't know what they've had to endure to attain their level of success. Besides, what God has given to you is not the same as what He has given the next person. You are unique, an original, and no one can be you but you.

I think one of the reasons we compare ourselves to others is self-consciousness and uncertainty; we don't know what the outcome will be if we take a step of faith and pursue our vision.

We think, "Well I can do better than that," or "If she can do it, I can do it." I encourage you to change your thought pattern to, "I can do all things through Christ who strengthens me," and "I can do it because God gave me the skills to do this task, and I will do it as unto Him and do it well." Don't add anyone else to the equation. God didn't give the vision to you for you to hold up measuring tape, but because He wanted you to get it done. And at the end, you can find comfort in knowing that you did it well. Colossians 3:23-24 reminds us of this, "Whatever you do, work at it with all your heart, as working for the Lord, not for human masters, since you know that you will receive an inheritance from the Lord as a reward. It is the Lord Christ you are serving."

<u>Study the following Scriptures: Philippians 4; Judges 8; 2 Corinthians 10:12</u>

How Long Are You Going to Wait?

Questions to consider:

1. Have you been measuring yourself against others?
2. If so, has comparison become a distraction? What can you do to overcome the spirit of comparison?
3. Is your vision clear enough to keep you focused on what you should be doing?
4. Comparison is a stumbling block and depending on how much we compare, we can find ourselves in a place where we're doing absolutely nothing. What can you do to prevent yourself from falling into a stalemate?

SEEK COUNSEL

When I finally decided to stop procrastinating with whatever excuse I thought plausible and begin my writing journey, one of the first things I did was to seek counsel. I had access to several authors, and I needed their guidance. Sure, I could write a book, but what comes next? Google can be a good friend when you're starting something new, but there's nothing like having someone who can encourage you, guide you and give you advice specific to your circumstance.

How Long Are You Going to Wait?

I have learned that when you step out on faith and pursue a vision that God has given to you, He will put people in your path to help you bring it to pass. However, you'll never know what or who is on the other side of your yes, if you don't put your yes into action.

An excellent example of not only listening to wise counsel, but taking heed to it can be found in Exodus 18:14–24. Moses had the weight of the entire community of Israel on his shoulders while he led them out of Egypt. His father-in-law took notice and advised him to get some help; the burden was too heavy and he shouldn't bear it alone. Moses took his advice and selected trustworthy men to serve as officials over different groups to assist Moses in taking care of the Israelites' affairs.

Moses could have listened to Jethro and allowed his advice to go in one ear and out of the other, but instead he took his advice and it made his load lighter. I don't think we're meant to go through life alone (see Ecclesiastes 4:11 and Matthew

18:20). Pursuing our purpose is easier with the help of trustworthy counsel.

If this vision you're pursuing is totally out of your comfort zone, the task of finding a mentor can probably seem a little daunting. How do you know who to trust? How will you know that this person will have your best interest at heart? This can be rather tricky and I wish I could tell you that things will work out fine and you'll find the perfect person the first go round, but I don't know that. Godly counsel will not contradict God's Word, but confirm it; s/he will encourage you, pray with you, and help you to stay focused when the journey gets rough. Even when you don't feel like it, you need to be reminded of the purpose—why you're doing what you're doing.

Find someone that you trust and, preferably, who has done what you're trying to do. She needs to be someone with godly wisdom that can pour into you and help guide you in your pursuit of purpose.

How Long Are You Going to Wait?

<u>Study the following Scriptures: Proverbs 16:22; Proverbs 19:20; Proverbs 20:18; Psalm 32:8</u>

Application

1. When you consider seeking counsel from someone wise, what does this person look like to you?
2. What do you need from them?
3. What role will they play in helping you pursue your purpose?

BALANCING IT ALL

You have your plan written down and you're so ready, but so many things get in the way. Mainly you never seem to have enough time. This is my favorite issue when I talk to others about pursuing their goals, because I can easily point out areas in their daily lives where they have time and can actually do something that will get them closer to doing what they truly desire to do.

But before we get into this whole issue of balance and finding time to pursue what you desire to do, take a moment to think about what you do with your day. Ponder these questions before you read any further:

- What time do you wake up in the morning?
- What do you do once you wake up?
- What do you do on your lunch breaks?
- What do you do when you get home?
- How many hours per day do you spend in front of the TV? On your phone? On the computer?
- What time do you go to bed at night, and what do you find yourself doing about thirty minutes before going to bed? Could you spend a few minutes emptying your mind by listing your goals/action items for the next day?

If you're like me and you have familial obligations, you have to be even more strategic about your time and how you can squeeze out an hour here and there to be productive in achieving this goal you have. So how do you make it work when it seems you have too many restraints?

I suggest writing down your daily obligations and creating a to-do list using a calendar. You may find that you are busy without purpose and have some tasks on your schedule that you can do without. Decide what deserves your time. Not everything is worthy of your time, attention, and resources.

I find that being intentional and prioritizing my time helps me stay focused. Whether through keeping a written list, using the calendar on your phone or e-mail, or some time management app, prioritize your daily tasks by putting the most important things at the top of the list so that you can take the necessary steps to see your vision through to fruition.

First Things First

It may be a cliché but there's a lot of truth to tackling the most important tasks first to make sure

How Long Are You Going to Wait?

they get done. Make them a priority. Even with a list, the most important things can fall to the wayside if we don't prioritize correctly. Think about it: By the end of the day, you're tired and worn out from the day's activities, and if taking a necessary step toward your purpose was at the end of the list, you'll put it off until tomorrow and the next day, then the day after, and you'll end up where you started. The very thing you need to do won't get done because you didn't make it a priority.

This reminds me of my commitment to go to the gym. I know very well that morning workouts are what works best for my schedule and for my body, but every now and again I'll hit the snooze button too many times and talk myself out of going with the rationale that I'll do it later that day. Later never comes, because by the end of the day, I have too many other obligations to tend to and gym time just won't fit in my schedule. Is this what you do with your goals? Assign a "later" timetable to them?

How Long Are You Going to Wait?

As I mentioned earlier, I waited many years before I wrote my first book. After the whole issue of waving my notepad in the air, three years passed before I actually sat down to put pen to paper. In 2011, this whole idea of writing came back to me again and weighed heavily on my heart. I prayed about it constantly. You see, I was hesitant because my first book was a devotional. Who was I to write a devotional? I'm not a pastor or a Christian with some type of public platform.

Every time I prayed about it, I felt like the sermon I heard that following Sunday was for me, but still I hesitated. One night after praying, I picked up my Bible and started reading Joshua 18:3, which says, "How long are you going to wait before you take possession of the land the Lord your God has already given you?" That Scripture text is actually about some tribes of Israel who had yet to take possession of the land that God already promised them. A few of the tribes had already fought and took possession of theirs while the

How Long Are You Going to Wait?

others were *waiting*. But God said to them, what are you waiting for? It's already yours, you just have to go get it. That Scripture spoke volumes to me because my *land* was these books; yet I was allowing fear and whispers of the enemy to hold me back.

You would think I would have started writing at that point, but I didn't. I verbally committed to it, but I didn't start writing because I had another set of excuses: the baby, needing a new computer, time, etc.

January 2012 rolled around and I was sitting in the living room on the floor playing with my daughter. I'd just finished watching a T. D. Jakes sermon on TV and another show broadcasted. I was only halfway listening until I heard the woman mention that she had a book she was supposed to write and she never did it. She had the title and the names of a few chapters, yet she didn't move. She went on to talk about how she'd gone to some conference and the pastor who was leading prayer called her forward and whispered the name of her book and chapter titles in her ear, but yet she didn't move. She continued to share how she has possibly missed out on so much because she never took action. One thing she mentioned stood out to me. She said we have to remember that when God gives us an assignment, it is for God's glory, and if we don't do it, our assignment can be reassigned. Wow!

That moment changed my thought process. I learned that God wants willing and available vessels. No longer did my fear, uncertainty, or worries about what other people would think or whether or not they would support me matter; the only thing that mattered was that God had already given me everything I needed to get started, I just needed to make myself available and do it.

Since stepping out on faith and putting pen to paper or fingers to keyboard, God has continually blessed and led my path. I'm reminded that there is someone waiting on the other side of my obedience, and though I get so much joy and peace out of writing, it is not about me. There is a story to tell or

How Long Are You Going to Wait?

a devotional to write that will encourage someone to grow closer to God.

So I ask you, *How long are you going to wait before you take possession of the land the Lord your God has already given you?*

About the author

In addition to reading and writing, Natasha enjoys reading, cooking, couponing, and spending her time with her husband and children. She has won the Readers' Choice award for her books, _The Life Your Spirit Craves_, _Love, Lies & Consequences_, and _The Life Your Spirit Craves for Mommies_.

Natasha believes that we were all created for purpose and inspires women to pursue their God-given purpose through her books and the How Long Are You Going to Wait Conference. Sign up for her monthly newsletter at www.natashafrazier.com for encouraging devotionals, current events and new releases.

Connect with Natasha:

Instagram @author_natashafrazier

Facebook @craves.2012

Twitter @author_natashaf

e-mail: Natasha@natashafrazier.com

It is my prayer that this book has encouraged you to take the next step in being all you were created to be. Please enjoy a few sample devotionals from *The Life Your Spirit Craves*.

DAY 1 - Your Purpose Has Been Predetermined

Isaiah 45:4 NLT
"And why have I called you for this work? Why did I call you by name when you did not know me? It is for the sake of Jacob my servant, Israel my chosen one.

In Isaiah 45, the passage teaches us that Cyrus was chosen by the Lord to restore his city and free the Lord's people. Cyrus was chosen before he even knew the Lord (v.4). This confirms that our purpose --our destiny-- is determined way before we meet the Lord, decide to follow Him and give our lives over to His purpose.

Verse 2 tells how the Lord will go before Cyrus to do His part in assisting Cyrus to accomplish the purpose God had predetermined. In verses 9-12, the Bible teaches us that we should not question or argue with the Lord about why we have been given the assignment in which He purposed for us. The Lord himself will guide our actions (v. 12) and that is assurance enough. You should know that oftentimes, it may not be revealed to you as to why the Lord has chosen you for a specific task especially when the task doesn't line up with your background or education. When this is the case, you have to truly rely on God's power and guidance in order to accomplish what He has called you to accomplish. The scripture reveals that God will go before you. You just have to follow. Remember that the assignment on your life is meant to give God glory and build up His people. Once these concepts are grasped, your assignments will be a "piece of cake."

So in this moment, I encourage you to first seek the Lord for your purpose because it was predetermined before you were born. Secondly, accept your purpose. Don't question or argue with the Lord about what He has called you to do or why He has called you to do it. Thirdly, receive the Lord's guidance and instruction. He already has the master plan. Lastly, serve with gladness.

Prayer for Today: Lord, I thank you for your greatness and your sovereignty. Lord, I thank you for your purpose for my life. I thank you because before I even came to know you, you already had a plan for me. I seek you today so that you may speak to my heart. I want to know you more and what you have purposed for me. Thank you for choosing me. Help me to serve you with joy and boldness. In Jesus' name, Amen.

For further study, read Isaiah 45:1-13.

DAY 1

JOURNAL

Life Questions/Application

1. For what purpose has the Lord called me?

2. Have I accepted this purpose for my life?

3. What can I do today that will cause me to be more faithful to this purpose?

DAY 2 - Ask, Seek, Knock

Matthew 7:7-8 NLT
Keep on asking, and you will receive what you ask for. Keep on seeking, and you will find. Keep on knocking, and the door will be opened to you. For everyone who asks, receives. Everyone who seeks, finds. And to everyone who knocks, the door will be opened.

Do you know your calling?
Do you know your purpose in the kingdom of God?
Have you even begun seeking God about it?

If not, now is a good time to start. The scripture tells us that when we ask something of the Lord, He will answer. Sometimes, the answer may not be immediate. That is why I believe the scripture says to keep on knocking and the door will be opened to you. Not only will God answer your prayer, He will open up many doors of opportunity for you to serve in His kingdom, allow you to serve His people and prepare you to be a blessing to them. If you keep seeking, you will find it.

I heard a sermon by Pastor Charles Jenkins that discussed "purpose" and "calling." He shared something that I now want to share with you. There are two callings on our lives: corporate and individual. He explained that we must first be connected to the corporate calling—the calling on our church body---which can be building a new church, community evangelism, etc. The individual calling is the specific calling that God has placed over each one of our lives to build up the kingdom and bring glory to God.

Before I accepted my assignment and calling to encourage others through the Word of God in writing, I would become very nervous and anxious whenever our pastor (or anyone) would mention the words "purpose" or "calling." Now, I get excited about hearing messages regarding this topic because the messages push me to go forward!

If you do not know your calling, I encourage you to take the following steps to begin this journey:

1. Accept the corporate calling of the ministry you are a part of. This is done by supporting the vision of the ministry through time and finances.
2. Seek the Lord to show you the calling that He has placed on your life (even before you were born). Pray. Study the Word of God. Fast. Consider what you are passionate about. I believe that passion = purpose.

No matter where you are in life, be encouraged and know that it is never too late to do what God has called you to do! Ask. Seek. Knock.

Prayer for Today: Father I thank you for being omniscient and sovereign! I magnify your name. I thank you that you created the purpose for my life even before you created me! I thank you right now for all that you're going to do through my life. I pray that you show me what it is that you want me to do and give me the courage to do it. I thank you for the manifestation of your power in my life, oh Lord! You are awesome and welcome to dwell within me. In Jesus' name, Amen.

> **For further study, please read Deuteronomy 6:18 and 2 Chronicles 15:2.**

DAY 2

JOURNAL

Life Questions/Application

1. What is the corporate calling of the ministry that I belong to?
   a. How have I supported the vision?
   b. What are ways that I can help further the vision of the ministry?

2. Lord please show me opportunities to serve in Your Kingdom. Help me to identify where you can use me and where I can be of service to You. Where is God calling me to serve Him?

DAY 13 - Who's Going With Me?

Exodus 33:15-16 NLT
Then Moses said, "If you don't personally go with us, don't make us leave this place. 16 How will anyone know that you look favorably on me—on me and on your people—if you don't go with us? For your presence among us sets your people and me apart from all other people on the earth."

In this passage, and throughout the book of Exodus, Moses is leading the Israelites into the Promised Land. The Lord has chosen and spoken to Moses to lead His people. The Lord gave Moses a series of tasks to complete on His behalf in front of the Israelites in order that they may believe that the Lord sent Moses. Moses spent much time with the Lord in prayer and communicating with God about what needed to be done. Moses spent much time in worship as well. Still, Moses needed more to accomplish his task. Moses needed God's glory! He needed God to not just give him instructions but to go with him! He knew that if the task God wanted Him to complete was to be completed, God needed to go with him. Everyone else needed to know and see that God was with him too.

Today as you contemplate what's before you, think about who is with you. Think about who gave you the instructions. Are you following the instructions? Did you ask the Lord to go with you?

Sometimes when you share your dreams, goals, or purpose with others, you will not get the response you're expecting. You may not receive an offer to help. You may not receive congratulatory remarks. You must remember that your purpose comes from God. You don't have to look to man to validate it. You cannot let others' opinions "put out your fire" or cause you to be any less excited about your dreams or what you have been called to do!

Let your daily prayer mirror Moses' words to the Lord in our key verse. Remember that God's presence sets you apart from everyone else!

Prayer for Today: Lord God, I honor you and give your name all of the Praise! O most worthy God, let your presence fill me today. Go with me on the path that you have set before me. Lord, I ask that you forgive me of my sins and my moments of doubt and hesitation. I have faith in you and your will for my life. Give me courage to be bold and step out on faith to do what you have called me to do. I love you and thank you for loving me in a way that only you can! In Jesus' name, Amen.

For further study, read the entire chapter of Exodus 33 and Proverbs 3:5-6.

DAY 13

JOURNAL

Life Questions/Application

1. Have I asked the Lord to let His presence rest and abide within me so that I may accomplish the task(s) that He has given me? Why or why not?

2. Am I seeking validation from others in regard to the assignment that God has given me? Am I afraid? Am I sure of what God has called me to do at this time in my life? What can I do so that I will be sure?

3. Have I been spending quality time reading and studying God's word? Am I giving God enough of my time so that I may hear His voice? How can I be sure of this?

To purchase a copy of The Life Your Spirit Craves, please visit www.natashafrazier.com

www.ingramcontent.com/pod-product-compliance
Lightning Source LLC
Chambersburg PA
CBHW021136300426
44113CB00006B/454